Franklin Leonard Pope

Ancestry of Captain Ebenezer Pope

Franklin Leonard Pope

Ancestry of Captain Ebenezer Pope

ISBN/EAN: 9783744670517

Printed in Europe, USA, Canada, Australia, Japan

Cover: Foto ©ninafisch / pixelio.de

More available books at **www.hansebooks.com**

CAPT. EBENEZER POPE.

GENEALOGICAL NOTES.

ELIZABETH, N. J. :
COOK & HALL. STEAM PRINTERS.

1882.

S ome years since, there fell into my hands a copy of a manuscript, said to be in the handwriting of my grandfather, Captain Ebenezer Pope, of Great Barrington, Mass., and in the possession of his eldest daughter, the late Mrs. Keziah (Pope) Kilbourn. This paper contained a record, extending from 1720 to 1740, of the names and dates of birth of the children of Capt. Pope's grandfather; but of the history, or even of the name of the progenitor of the family whose record had been thus preserved, nothing definite appears to have been heretofore known by any of the descendants now living.

During the past year (1881), availing myself of the opportunity afforded by a short respite from the ordinary occupations of a somewhat busy life, I undertook the task of tracing the early history of our immediate family in this country, and especially the ancestry of Capt. Ebenezer. Having reason to conjecture that this branch of the family migrated, during the last century, from some portion of the Old Plymouth Colony, I made a careful examination of the records of some of the older towns in that part of Massachusetts, especially those of Plymouth, Sandwich and Old Dartmouth. I also visited the two last named places, and made myself familiar with many of the ancient localities referred to in the records.

Although the time which I was enabled to devote

to these investigations was necessarily brief, I was n-
ertheless fortunate enough to find much material of
terest and value, more or less directly relating to t'
object of my search, and it affords me pleasure to
able to present in a condensed form, from material
my possession, a nearly complete outline of the gene--
ogy of Captain Ebenezer Pope in the direct line fr
the emigrant ancestor.

THOMAS POPE[1], the ancestor of our family in Am
ica, was born in 1608. It is not known from whe
he emigrated to this country, or in what year, but
his name first appears in the records at Plymouth
1631, it is probable that he came about 1630, or so-
after he was of age. He m. Jan. 28, 1637, ANN,
of Gabriel and Catherine Fallowell of Plymouth, a
by her had *Hannah*, b. 1639. When this wife d.
not known, but he m. 2d, May 29, 1646, SARAH, d.
John and Sarah Jenney of Plymouth. Jenney was
prominent man in the Colony; he came in 1673 fr
Leyden, but was originally from Norwich, Eng. T
children of Thomas and Sarah were : *Seth*, b. Jan.
1648; *Susannah*, 1649; *Sarah*, 1650; *Thomas*, Mar. !
1651; *Joanna* ; *Isaac* ; *John*, Mar. 15, 1673, and p
haps *Patience*. Of these, Sarah m. Nov. 13, 16:
Samuel, s. of Thomas Hinckley, Esq., Governor of
Plymouth Colony from 1658 until its union with M
sachusetts in 1692. Susannah m. 1666, Jacob Mitch
and with her husband and brother John was killed
Dartmouth by Philip's warriors in 1675. Thomas li-
many years in Plymouth, and appears from the reco
to have been a respected and worthy citizen. He r
ertheless fell under the displeasure of the authorit

and in 1670, was fined ten shillings, as the record says, "for villifying the ministry." Not long after this occurrence I find him at Dartmouth, but the precise date of his removal thither cannot be ascertained. His will is dated " 12–5=1683," and it is probable that his death took place not long afterwards. The place of his burial is not known.

SETH[2], eldest son of Thomas of Plymouth, b. Jan. 13, 1648, probably went to Dartmouth with his father about 1670. He m. DEBORAH —— about 1674, and had *John*, Oct. 23, 1675 ; *Thomas*, Sept. 1, 1677 ; *Susannah*, Jul. 31, 1681 ; *Sarah*, Feb. 16, 1683 ; *Mary*, Sep. 11, 1686 ; *Seth*, Apr. 5, 1689 ; *Hannah*, Dec. 14, 1693 ; *Elnathan*, Aug. 15, 1694, and *Lemuel*, Feb. 21, 1696. Seth and his brother Isaac were among the proprietors of Dartmouth, as appears from the confirmatory deed of Governor Bradford in 1694. Seth was an extensive landholder and merchant in D., and became a very prominent, influential and wealthy citizen. He was the first magistrate of the town, and also represented it in the General Court of the Old Colony at Plymouth, 1689-90. His descendants have been very numerous, and not a few of them are still to be found in the southeastern portion of Massachusetts. His 1st wife, Deborah, the mother of all his children, d. Feb 19, 1711 ; he m. 2d, Rebecca —— who survived him and d. Jan. 25, 1741. Seth d. Mar. 17, 1727, æ 79, and was buried in the ancient graveyard at Acushnet, east of the "Head of the River," three miles from New Bedford, Mass. A thrifty pine tree grows upon his grave, which is marked by a quaintly inscribed and sculptured memorial stone. His homestead was one-fourth of a mile distant, on the road leading to Fair

Haven village, east of the river. The house w s
burned by the British troops during their expediti
against New Bedford in 1778, it being at that tin -
occupied by Col. Seth Pope, his grandson, who was a..
active patriot leader, and had incurred the hostility ..
his tory neighbors.

John[3], eldest s. of Seth of Dartmouth, b. in D., Oc:.
23, 1675, settled in Sandwich on an estate purchased t ;
his father from John Dexter, the original deed of whic...
dated Feb. 3, 1700, is yet in the possession of one of tl
descendants of the Dartmouth ancestor. He m., probab:
in 1700, ELIZABETH, d. of Elisha and Patience Bourne
Sandwich, and had *Seth*, Jan. 3, 1701 ; *Deborah*, Jan.
1703 ; *Sarah*, Mar. 25, 1706 ; *Elizabeth*, Jan. 3, 1707
Thomas, 1709, and *Mary*, Dec. — 1713. His 1st wi:
d. Apr. 15, 1715, and he m. 2d, EXPERIENCE JENKINS, (
Barnstable, and by her had *Ezra*, Apr. 3, 1719, *Joanne*
Mar. 3, 1722, and *Charles*, Feb. 28, 1725. John d. No
18, 1725 ; his burial-place is marked by a moss-grow
slab in the old graveyard in Sandwich village. Tl
house built for him by his father about 1700 is sti
standing, although enlarged and somewhat modernized.

SETH[4], eldest s. of John of Sandwich, b. Jan. 3, 170:
m. Jun. 22, 1719, JERUSHA, d. of Gershom and Mehetab -
Tobey of Sandwich, and had *Ichabod*, Sep. 5, 1720, wi
d. young ; *Elizabeth*, Oct. 3, 1721 ; *Deborah*, Feb. 2
1725 ; *John*, Apr. 24, 1727 ; *Mehetable*, May 27, 1729
Seth, Apr. 19, 1731 ; *Gershom*, Dec. 18, 1733 ; *Elnathu*
Aug. 16, 1735, and *Ichabod*, Jan. 27, 1740. Seth live
in Sandwich for many years after his marriage, and was
prominent and much respected townsman. He was fr
quently chosen by his fellow-citizens to fill positions

official trust; was collector of taxes in 1726, pound-keeper in 1731-7, and surveyor of highways in 1739-41 and 1745-8. In 1749, all his daughters having married, and his eldest living son John having become of age, he removed from Sandwich to Lebanon, Conn., where he bought a farm, upon which he lived until 1759, when he sold out and probably removed thence. I have as yet ascertained nothing of his subsequent history.

SETH[5], the sixth child of Seth of Sandwich, b. Apr. 19, 1731, was, according to family tradition, the father of Captain EBENEZER of Alford and Great Barrington. I have good reason to suppose that the 2d wife of Seth, and mother of Capt. E., was a daughter of Ebenezer Bacon, of Barnstable, b. Mar. 15, 1705, who m Lydia Lothrop, a descendant of Rev. John Lothrop, an eminent divine, and graduate of Oxford, who came in 1634 or 1635, and was pastor of the the church at Scituate and afterwards at Barnstable. Ebenezer B. was a great-grandson of Nathaniel Bacon of Barnstable, a man of great ability and moral worth, very prominent in the public affairs of the Colony, especially during the twenty years preceding his death in 1673. He was likewise a great-grandson of Governor Thomas Hinckley, before mentioned. Mrs. Lydia (Lothrop) Bacon was admitted into the church in Lebanon in 1748, and d. there Jan. 2, 1791, æ 78.

I shall be grateful for any additional genealogical data which may hereafter be furnished me, relating either to the family of Seth[5] of Connecticut, or to any of the descendants of Capt. Ebenezer of Great Barrington, as I may, perhaps, at some future time undertake to prepare a more detailed and complete history of the family.

FRANK L. POPE.

Elizabeth, N. J., Feb. 1, 1882.

NOTICE OF SOME OF THE DESCENDANTS OF JOSEPH POPE, OF SALEM.

BY HENRY WHEATLAND.

This account is only a compilation of a few facts that have been gathered from various sources, without any extended research, and should be considered merely as *materials for a history of this family*, which, I trust, some future antiquary will, ere long, be induced to prepare. The compiler desires notice of any error or omission.

JOSEPH POPE, the progenitor of the various families of the name now residing in this vicinity, is said to be the son of Robert Pope, of Yorkshire, England. He came to this country in the "Mary and John," of London, in 1634, was recorded a Church Member before 1636, made a Freeman in 1637, had lands granted in 1637 and at other times in that portion of Salem now known as West Danvers, and some of it bordering on Ipswich River. He and his wife Gertrude were before the court in 1658 for attending Quaker Meetings, and in 1662 were excommunicated for their adherence to the opinions of that sect. He died about 1667. His will, dated Sept. 10, 1666, mentions wife Gertrude executrix. In court, 27. 4, 1667.

The following children are recorded among the baptisms of the First Church, in Salem :—

2. Damaris,[2] bap. 1643, 22. 2; mar. Joshua Buffum.

3. Hannah,[2] bap. 1645, 20. 5.

4. Hannah,[2] bap. 1648, 26. 1; m. Caleb Buffum, 26 March, 1672; had son Caleb, b. 14th May, 1673; Robert, b. 1. 10, 1675.

5. George,[2] bap. 1649, 8. 5.

6. Joseph,[2] bap. 1650, 27. 8. (*Vide infra.*)

7. Benjamin,[2] bap. 1653, 17. 2. (*Vide infra.*)

8. Samuel,[2] bap. 1656, 18. 3. (*Vide infra.*)

9. Enos,[2] mentioned in his father's will, not recorded among the baptisms.

II. GENERATION.

(6)

JOSEPH POPE,[2] bap. 1650. 27. 8, a farmer, lived at "The Village;" m. Bethseda Folger, daughter of Peter Folger,[*] of Nantucket, one of the first settlers on that island, and in consequence of his valuable services at that period, his name has always been held in high esteem. Abiah, the sister of Bethseda, mar. Josiah Franklin, and was the mother of Dr. Benjamin Franklin, a name that stands high in the annals of science.

[*] See an account of the Folger family in N. E. Hist. and Gen. Reg., vol. 16, p. 269.

Joseph Pope died in 1712, having had the following children : —

10. Joseph,[3] b.　　　; d. young.

11. Bethseda,[3] b. Ap. 9, 1688; d. unm.

12. Gertrude,[3] b. Aug. 27, 1685; m.

m. Ebenezer, third son of Thomas Flint, a farmer, lived in North Reading, born April 6, 1683, and died 1767; had six children, Nathaniel, Ebenezer, Lois, Nathan, Amos, Eunice. See "Flint's Genealogy," p. 13.

13. Joseph,[3] b. June 16, 1687. (*Vide infra*.)

14. Enos,[3] b. June 6, 1690. (*Vide infra*.)

15. Eleazer,[3] b. Dec. 4, 1693. (*Vide infra*.)

16. Jerusha,[3] b. April 1, 1695; m. July 9, 1713, George Flint, son of George and Elizabeth (Putnam) Flint, b. April 1, 1686; she died June 29, 1781; had seven children, namely, Susanna, Jerusha, Elizabeth, Abigail, George, Eliezer, Hannah. See "Flint Genealogy," p. 15.

17. Nathaniel,[3] b. Nov. 20, 1679. (*Vide infra*.)

(7)

BENJAMIN POPE,[2] bap. 1653, 17. 2, a farmer; mar. Damaris, dau. of Samuel and Hannah Shattuck,* of

Salem, b. Nov. 11, 1653; administration on estate granted to his son Benjamin April 13, 1702; children, —

18. Benjamin.[3] (*Vide infra*.)

19. Samuel,[3] husbandman, lived in "The Village." Inventory of estate returned Sept. 26, 1753, nephew John Pope, administrator. Probably no issue.

20. Ebenezer,[3] died without issue in 1717; administration on his estate to his brother, July 12, 1718.

21. Jerome,[3] mentioned in 1718, having been absent a long time at sea, and supposed to be lost.

(8)

SAMUEL POPE,[2] bapt. 1656, 18. 3, a mariner; m. Jan. 28, 1685. Exer-

his connection with this persecution. see "Bessie's Collection of the Sufferings of the People called Quakers," "Bishop's New England Judged," "Fox's Journal," and elsewhere. Shattuck went to England and presented the subject of the suffering to the notice of Charles II., and by the assistance of Edward Burroughs obtained, Sept. 19, 1661, "a mandamus," commanding the magistrates and ministers in New England " to forbear to proceed any farther " against the people called Quakers, — and he was appointed agent to carry this mandamus to New England. The General Court, Nov. 27, 1661, accordingly passed an order suspending the laws against the Quakers, and the jailers were directed to release those who were in custody. Thus, principally through his instrumentality, terminated one of the most extraordinary persecutions that this country ever witnessed. Afterwards he was permitted to live in Salem undisturbed. He seems to have been a man independent in his opinion, and unwilling to submit to oppression. — See " Shattuck Memorials," by L. Shattuck, p. 361.

* Samuel Shattuck, son of widow Damaris, was born in England about 1620. He was a hatter in Salem, where he died June 6, 1689. He was one of those who suffered persecution for being called a Quaker. For an account of

cise Smith, dau. of John and Margaret Smith,* of Salem. Children, —

22. Damaris, b. Feb. 1686–7 ; d.
1½ years after.

23. Samuel,[3] b. June 11, 1689.

24. Margaret,[3] b. Oct. 21, 1691.

25. Enos,[3] b. Feb. 1, 1694–5.

26. Hannah.[3] b. Feb. 17, 1696–7 ;
m. Nov. 25, 1714, Isaac Hacker, and
had Hannah, b. Oct. 24, 1715 ; Sarah,
b. Aug. 29, 1717 ; Eunice, b. Jan.
24, 1719 ; Isaac, b. July 2. 1722 ;
Jeremiah, b. May 27, 1725 ;† Isaac, b.

* John and Margaret Smith were among
those who were persecuted for their adherence
to the opinions of the Quakers. Bishop's
" New England Judged " contains an account.
of these persecutions, also letters addressed
to Governor John Endecott, one signed by
John Smith and delivered to him shortly after
the death of Mary Dyer in 1660: another signed by Mary Trask and Margaret Smith. dated.
" From your House of Correction, where we
have been unjustly restrained. from our Children and Habitations: one of us above ten
months, and the other about eight. and where
we are yet continued by you. Oppressors that
know no shame. *Boston*, the 21st of the 20th
month, 1660." Margaret Smith died at Salem,
11. 11, 1677. Inventory of estate of John
Smith, deceased, was appraised 16th April,
1680.

† Isaac Hacker, known as Master Hacker,
was a son of this Jeremiah, and a native of
Salem. He died very suddenly in September,
1818, aged sixty-eight. He was a much respected member of the Society of Friends,
and an instructor of youth for about forty
years. He was the master of the " West
School " in Salem, now known as " Hacker
School," from its institution in 1785, till with-
in two or three years of his decease. This
long continuance in the situation is the strong-
est testimony of the public approbation and
respect.

Nov. 28, 1727 ; Hannah, b. May 16,
1729 ; Isaac, b. March 4, 1730.

27. Elizabeth,[3] b. May 23, 1698.

28. Eunice,[3] b. Aug. 12, 1700 ; m.
Nov. 14, 1728, Joseph Cook, — had
Eunice, b. Sept. 6, 1729 ; Hannah,
b. June 19, 1732 ; John, b. July 22,
1735.

29. Ruth,[3] b. March 11, 1705 ; d.
July 6, 1705.

This is, without doubt, the Samuel
Pope who married, in 1709, Martha,
the widow of William Beane, jr., and
dau. of Samuel and Martha (Haw-
kins) Robinson, b. 1673, 11. 20. She
m. Joseph Winslow, and by him had
Joseph, b. Feb. 21, 1695–6 ; m. secondly, Oct. 29, 1702, William Beane,
and had William, b. July 2, 1703,
Caleb, b. Feb. 22, 1704–5 ; m. third-
ly, Samuel Pope, and had the following, who were baptized at First
Church, Salem.

30. Martha,[3] bap. May 20, 1711.

31. Mary,[3] bap. Aug. 30, 1713.

32. Susanna,[3] bap. June 30, 1717.

33. Abigail,[3] bap. Dec. 31, 1727,
adult.

Samuel Pope died before 1735.

III. GENERATION.

(13)

JOSEPH POPE,[3] b. June 16, 1687,
a farmer, resided at " The Village ";
m. Feb. 7, 1715–16. Mehitable Putnam, dau. of John and Hannah Putnam, b. July 20, 1695. Will signed
March 25, 1755, mentions wife Me-

hitable, and appoints sons Ebenezer and Eleazer executors. In Court, Oct. 13, 1755. Children, —

34. Joseph,[4] bap. Sept. 1, 1717 ; m. Hannah Shaw, of Salem, Oct. 7, 1743 ; was living at Pomfret, Conn., in 1755.

35. Mehitable,[4] bap. May 3, 1719 ; m. April 18, 1841, Joseph Gardner, son of Abel and Sarah (Porter) Gardner, and had Joseph, Mehitable, Nathaniel, Eunice.

36. Hannah,[4] bap. Sept. 3, 1721 ; m. June 30, 1739, Israel Putnam, son of Joseph and Elizabeth (Porter) Putnam, b. Jan. 7, 1717–18 ; d. May 19, 1790. In 1739, removed from Salem to Pomfret, Conn. ; having purchased a tract of land, he applied himself successfully to agriculture. He died May 19, 1790, widely known as a celebrated major-general in the Continental Army during the American Revolution. She died in 1764.

37. Nathaniel,[4] bap. May 17, 1724. (Vide infra.)

38. Eunice,[4] bapt. April 30, 1727 ; m. October, 1745, Col. John Baker, of Ipswich. She died at Ipswich, January, 1821, aged ninety-four. A contemporary says, "she was a remarkable woman, and retained her faculties to the last. She was a connection of the late General Putnam, and was full of the same ardor that possessed him."

39. Mary,[4] bapt. May 31, 1730 ; m. Nov. 28, 1748, Samuel Williams, of Pomfret, Conn.

40. Ebenezer,[4] bapt. June 9, 1734. (Vide infra.)

41. Eleazer,[4] bapt. Nov. 14, 1736. (Vide infra.)

42. Elizabeth,[4] bapt. October 14, 1739.

(14)

ENOS POPE,[3] b. June 6, 1690, a clothier ; lived near the Fowler house on Boston street. In 1718, he built the house now occupied by Mr. John G. Wilkins, 92 Boston street, where he, his son Enos, and grandson Enos carried on the same business for upwards of a century ; m. 1715, 1 mo. 17, Margaret Smith, b. March 18, 1691, a daughter of George and Hannah Smith, of Salem, who was the son of John and Margaret Smith. (See No. 8.) He died Feb. 24, 1765 ; administration granted to Enos Pope, his son, Oct. 25, 1766 ; had, —

43. Enos,[4] b. 9 mo. 18, 1721. (Vide infra.)

44. Margaret,[4] b. 6. 7, 1723 ; d. 25th of same month.

45. Joseph,[4] b. 5. 29, 1724 ; d. 23d of ye 12 mo. following.

46. Benjamin,[4] b. 10. 3, 1725 ; d. 2d of ye 11 mo. following.

47. Joseph,[4] b. 4. 5, 1728 ; d. 14. 6 mo. following.

48. Seth,[4] b. 11. 23, 1730 ; d. 5 of 8 mo. following.

49. John,[4] b. 9. 17, 1732 ; d. 18 of ye 5 mo. following.

50. Hannah,[4] b. 4. 19, 1734 ; d. 27 of ye 5 mo. following.

(15)

ELEAZER POPE,[3] b. Dec. 4, 1693, cordwainer, m. April 3, 1718, Hannah Buffington. He died 2. 5 m°. 1734. Inventory of his estate taken Oct. 15, 1734, including dwelling-house, land, and shop (near the Elm tree on Boston street, Salem). Hannah Pope, his widow, administratrix.

51. Stephen.[4] (*Vide infra.*)

(17)

NATHANIEL POPE,[3] b. Nov. 20, 1679, a blacksmith, of Salem; mar. Dec. 17, 1703, Prisca Chatwell, dau. of Nicholas and Sara Chatwell, b. 22. 2, 1679; died   . The widow, April 14, 1711, m. John Meachum, of Enfield, Hampshire county, and removed to that place. Children,—

52. Mary,[4] b. Feb. 27, 1704–5; m. Nathaniel Parsons, of Enfield, husbandman.

53. Sarah,[4] b.   ; m. Nathaniel Meachum, of Enfield, husbandman.

(18)

BENJAMIN POPE,[3] husbandman, m. June 24, 1710, Sarah Smith, of Cape Ann. Inventory of estate returned Nov. 29, 1769, son John Pope 'administrator.

54. Mary,[4] b. January, 1711–12; died Sept. 8, 1712.

55. John,[4] b. March 16, 1713–14. (*Vide infra.*)

(23)

SAMUEL POPE,[3] b. at Salem, 1689, 4. 11; d. 1769, 9. 21; m. Sarah

Estes, of Lynn, November 20, 1714; born at Salem, 1693, 3. 5; d. 1773, 1. 10. Children,—

56. Elizabeth,[4] b. 1716, 4. 16; d. 1716, 5. 5.

57. Robert,[4] b. 1717, 6. 9. (*Vide infra.*)

58. Ebenezer,[4] b. 1719–20, 1. 23. (*Vide infra.*)

59. Estes,[4] b. 1721–2, 12. 18; d. 1725–6, 11. 16.

60. Philadelphia,[4] b. 1723–4, 12. 26; d. 1750, 8. 3.

61. Sarah,[4] b. 1726, 5. 2; d. 1768, 4. 4.

62. Ruth,[4] b. 1728–9, 1. 6; d. 1764, 1. 30.

63. Samuel,[4] b. 1731, 7. 27.

64. Henry,[4] b. 1733, 6. 14; d. the same night.

65. Hannah,[4] b. 1734, 7. 20.

IV. GENERATION.

(37)

NATHANIEL POPE,[4] farmer, resided at "The Village." Baptized May 17, 1724; m. Mary, dau. of Jasper Swinnerton, b. 1728; d. Dec. 20, 1773. He m., secondly, Dec. 23, 1784, Sarah, dau. of Rev. Peter and Deborah (Hobart) Clark, of Danvers. She was born Dec. 18, 1738; d. Feb. 12, 1802. He died in Nov. 1800, and administration on estate granted to Amos and Elijah Pope, March 2, 1801. Children,—

66. Mary,[5] b. Dec. 12, 1748; m. June 4, 1777, Aaron Gilbert.

1*

67. Eunice,[5] b. Feb. 19, 1751 ; m. Sept. 16, 1773, James Putnam.

68. Nathaniel,[5] b. March 22, 1753 ; d. unmarried, Feb. 10, 1778.

69. Rebecca,[5] b. April 16, 1755 ; m. Jan. 27, 1784, Jonathan Proctor, of Dunstable.

70. Hannah,[5] b. Aug. 21, 1757 ; d. at the age of twenty-one years.

71. Jasper,[5] b. Oct. 10, 1759 ; d. at the age of nineteen years and two months.

72. Ruth,[5] b. Nov. 7, 1761 ; d. at the age of two years.

73. Zephaniah,[5] b. May 6, 1764 ; d. unmarried, aged thirty-two.

74. Elijah,[5] b. Jan. 28, 1766. (*Vide infra.*)

75. Mehitable,[5] b. April 3, 1768, d. June 2, 1837 ; m. Caleb Oakes, of Danvers. Was the mother of William Oakes, of Ipswich, a very distinguished botanist, who was born in Danvers July 1, 1799 ; graduated at Harvard College in 1820 ; died July 31, 1848. See an obituary notice in American Journal of Science and Arts, vol. 7 (Second Series), p. 138.

76. Amos,[5] b. Feb. 20, 1772. (*Vide infra.*)

(40)

EBENEZER POPE,[4] bap. June 9, 1734 ; d. Nov. 4, 1802 ; m. October 1754, Sarah, dau. of John and Mary (Eaton) Pope. See No. 113. She died in South Reading October 12, 1832, aged 94 years. Children. —

77. Lucretia,[5] m.   Poole, of South Reading.

78. John.[5]   (*Vide infra.*)

79. Eben.[5]   (*Vide infra.*)

80. Lucy.[5]

81. Oliver.[5]   (*Vide infra.*)

82. Mary,[5] m. Ananiah Parker, of South Reading.

83. Elizabeth,[5] m. Thomas Swan, of South Reading.

84. Jane.[5]

85. Abraham Gould.[5] Removed to Maine, married and died there.

(41)

ELEAZER POPE.[4] bap. Nov. 14, 1736 ; m. Nanny Putnam, July 7, 1757.

86. Eleazer,[5] b. Feb. 4, 1758 ; m. April, 1780, Mary Gardner.

87. Rebecca,[5] b. Dec. 31, 1759 ; m. Nov. 28, 1781, Thomas Gardner.

88. Molly.[5] bap. April 16, 1762.

89. Joseph,[5] b. June 28, 1764 ; m. Susanna Marsh, March 20, 1789.

90. Mehitable.[5] bap. Nov. 8, 1767.

91. Nanna.[5] bap. July 24, 1769 ; m. Jesse Leavenworth, of Danville, Feb. 20, 1791.

92. Allen.[5] bap. July 12, 1772.

93. Huldah,[5] bap. Dec. 5, 1773.

94. Perley Putnam.[5] bap. July 9, 1775 ; m. Jan. 13, 1799, Rebecca, dau. of Hezekiah and Esther (Coose) Flint, of North Reading ; removed to Danville, Vermont.

95. Betsey.[5] b. Aug. 13, 1777 ; m. Sept. 25, 1795, Deacon Simeon Flint, who was born in North Reading Jun-

24, 1775; removed to Danville, Vt., 1799, and thence in 1810 to Shipton, Canada East, where he died July 3, 1857, having had nine children. (See "Flint Genealogy," p. 46.)

96. Jasper,[5] b. Jan. 1. 1780. (*Vide infra.*)

97. William Walton,[5] bap. Oct. 31. 1784; d. unm., at Salem, aged twenty-one.

The members of this family removed principally to Vermont.

(43)

Enos Pope,[4] b. at Salem, 1721, 9. 18; d. March 12. 1813,—the oldest man in the town of Salem, a clothier by occupation, and lived in the same house which his father built. He married Lydia, dau. of Joshua and Buffum, of Salem; b. Oct. 10, 1726; d. Oct. 15. 1781. Children,—

98. Lydia,[5] b. 1750, 1. 28.

99. Margaret,[5] b. 1752, 6. 5.

100. Eunice,[5] b. 1755. 5. 2; d. Sept. 1819. unmarried.

101. Hannah,[5] b. 1757, 4. 2; d. at Salem. 1836, 9. 16.

102. Enos,[5] b. 1759, 4. 27. a clothier; lived in the house built and occupied by his grandfather Enos, also by his father Enos; died unmarried Nov. 24, 1838.

103. Damaris,[5] b. 1761, 8. 11.

(51)

Stephen Pope,[4] b.   ; d. Oct. 9, 1765, cordwainer; resided in Salem, near the Elm Tree on Boston-street; m. Mary, dau. of Joshua and

Buffum, b. July 8, 1723, d. July 1788. Children,—

104. Hannah,[5] b. May 31, 1746; d. May 20, 1840, æt. ninety-three; m. Thomas Nichols, of Somersworth, N. H., and Salem, son of David and Hannah (Gaskell) Nichols; died at Salem December, 1805, aged sixty years.

105. Mary,[5] b. March 24, 1748; d. young.

106. Eleazer,[5] b. March 21, 1751. (*Vide infra.*)

107. Gertrude,[5] b. Oct. 19, 1753; d. 1833, 9. 24.

108. Folger,[5] b. Feb. 14. 1756. (*Vide infra.*)

109. Stephen,[5] b. June 6, 1759; d. young.

110. Sarah,[5] b. Aug. 20, 1761; d. 1841, 10. 18; m. David Nichols, brother of Thomas, and lived at Berwick, Me.

111. Joshua,[5] b. Nov. 24, 1763. (*Vide infra.*)

112. James,[5] b. Dec. 16, 1765, (*Vide infra.*)

(55)

John Pope,[4] b. March 16, 1713–14; m. April 22, 1736, Mary Eaton, of Lynn; a yeoman; lived in Danvers. His will was dated March 20, 1756. In court, June 5, 1756, Mary Pope, the widow, was appointed executrix. This is probably the widow Mary Pope, who m. Jacob Sawyer, of Reading, April, 1758. Children.—

113. Eben,[5] probably died young.
114. Sarah,[5] d. 1832; m. Eben Pope. (See No. 40.)
115. Mary,[5] m. William Deadman, jr., of Salem, in 1758.
116. Elizabeth,[5] m. Isaac Needham, of Salem, Jan. 9, 1769.
117. Lydia,[5] m. Sept. 16. 1762, Thomas Flint, who was born in North Reading Oct. 3, 1733, and died about 1800; a physician; removed to Maine in 1770, and settled in Nobleborough on the Damariscotta River; she died in 1784, having had ten children. See "Flint Genealogy," p. 32.

(57)

ROBERT POPE,[4] b. 1717, 6. 9; d. at Falmouth, Casco Bay, 1776, 2. 22; m. Phebe. She was b. 1716, 11 8.
118. John,[5] b. at Boston, 1740, 10. 19. (Vide infra.)
119. Robert,[5] b. at Boston, 1741, 10. 14; d. 1742, 6. 9.
120. Elijah,[5] b. at Boston, 1742, 12. 23.
121. Abigail,[5] b. at Boston, 17-3, 12. 9.
122. Phebe,[5] b. at Boston, 17-5, 8. 7; d. 1745, 8. 20.
123. Phebe,[5] b. at Boston, 1746, 8. 5; d. 1747, 11. 9.
124. Robert Brown,[5] b. 1748, 2. 5; d. 1748, 6. 4.
125. Joseph,[5] b. 1748, 11. 19.
126. Elizabeth,[5] b. 1759, 2. 20.
127. Phebe,[5] b. 1751, 7.
128. Robert,[5] b. 1754, 9. 3.

(58)

EBENEZER POPE,[4] b. 1719-20, 1. 23; m. Elizabeth, b. 1717-18, 12. 5.
129. Elizabeth,[5] b. 1745, 7. 6; d. 1745, 7. 22.
130. Robert,[5] b. 1746, 7. 1; d. 1767, 8. 11.
131. Ebenezer,[5] b. 1748-9, 11. 4; d. 1749, 2. 16.
132. Fourth child dead born 1750, 4. 4.
133. Estes,[5] b. 1757, 10. 2.

V. GENERATION.

(74)

ELIJAH POPE,[5] b. Jan. 28, 1766; d. Feb. 16, 1846; m. June 20, 1791, Hannah Putnam. She died Sept. 10, 1844; lived in Danvers. Children,—
134. Nathaniel,[6] b. Aug. 2. 1792. (Vide infra.)
135. Hannah,[6] b. Sept. 29, 1794; m. Francis Fletcher, of Dunstable, and had three daughters.—Rachel, Hannah, and Mary.
136. Betsey,[6] b. Feb. 18, 1797; m. Samuel Putnam, son of Eleazer Putnam, and removed to Brooklyn, N. Y.
137. Mary,[6] b. April 19, 1799; d. June 25, 1823, unmarried.
138. Jasper,[6] b. July 14, 1802. (Vide infra.)
139. Phebe,[6] b. Nov. 8, 1807; d. Aug. 25, 1830.
140. Elijah,[6] b. July 13, 1809. (Vide infra.)

(76)

- AMOS POPE,[5] born at Danvers, Feb. 20, 1772; d. at Danvers, Jan. 26, 1837; m. at Danvers, Jan. 16, 1806, Sarah Goodale, b. April 19, 1773; d. Sept. 7, 1832. The subject of the preceding article. Children,—

141. Zephaniah,[6] b. Dec. 15, 1807.

142. Eunice,[6] b. May 30, 1810; d. Oct. 20, 1834.

(78)

JOHN POPE,[5] d. at Salem, December, 1820. æt. sixty-three, a baker by trade, also a soldier of the Revolution. His wife, Ruth Newhall, born at Lynnfield, died at Salem; December, 1810, æt. forty-nine. He married, secondly, Lydia M. Tunnison. Children,—

143. Sally,[6] d. March, 1808. æt. twenty-seven.

144. Ruth,[6] m. Archelaus Fuller.

145. John,[6] d. abroad.

146. George,[6] d. at Salem, Aug. 31, 1832.

147. Sophia,[6] m. Oliver Parker.

148. Thomas S.,[6] d. Nov. 29, 1844, aged forty, at Salem; m. Rebecca Spencer, of Beverly. Children living in Salem.

149. Eben,[6] d. Sept. 1811. æt. eighteen.

150. Sarah,[6] m.   Deland.

(79)

EBEN POPE,[5] of Salem, baker, b. in Danvers, July 7, 1759; d. in Salem Feb. 14, 1821, æt. sixty-two. He married August, 1779, Mehitable

Carroll, dau. of Capt. Samuel and Mehitable (Williams) Carroll. She died in 1784. He m., secondly, January 31, 1790, Lydia, widow of James Hayes, of Salem, and dau. of William Darling, of Cambridge. She died Feb. 16, 1816, aged sixty-two.

151. Samuel C.[6] (*Vide infra.*)

(81)

OLIVER POPE,[5] resided some time in South Reading, afterwards moved to Salem, and resided on Dean street; d. Oct. 23, 1825, æt. sixty; m. 1st,   ; secondly, Jan. 26, 1819, widow Mary Holman, dau. of James and Sarah Fabens. She died at Salem, Jan. 26, 1854, æt. 73½ years. Children,—

152. Oliver,[6] resides in one of the Western States.

153. Lois.[6]

154. Lucretia.[6]

155. Samuel,[6] m. Nov. 2, 1823, Betsey Newhall.

156. John,[6] resides in South Reading; m. Sept. 11, 1820, Harriet Holman.

(96)

JASPER POPE, a tailor, resided in Salem and sometimes in Danvers; born in Danvers, Jan. 1, 1780; died March 2, 1850; m. Dec. 14, 1804, at Salem, Abigail Lander (b. June 11, 1782, in Salem; d. Jan. 12, 1837). Children,—

157. Abigail Lander, b. at Salem, June 14, 1805; d. at Worcester, July 10, 1861.

158. William Allen, b. April 30, 1808, at Salem; d. 1817.

159 Ann Putnam, b. March 29, 1810, at Salem; d. at Danvers, April 12, 1837.

160. Caroline, b. Nov. 3, 1811, at Salem; d. July 22, 1845, at Danvers.

161. Matilda, b. July 18, 1814, at Salem.

162. Horatio Gates, b. at Salem, Dec. 7, 1815; engaged in business in Boston, resides in Malden.

(106)

ELEAZER POPE,[5] resided in Salem, yeoman, b. March 21, 1751; d. 1818, 2. 5; m. Esther, dau. of Jonathan Buxton, b. 1760, 12. 9; d. 1818, 10. 17.

163. Mary,[6] b. 1788, 7. 16; m. Joshua Buxton, of Danvers, who was born July 17, 1785, and had Joshua, b. Oct. 14, 1817; Mary Jane, b. Oct. 20, 1821, and Henry Varney, b. July 23, 1824.

164. Esther,[6] b. 1790, 10. 27; m. Henry Grant, of Salem.

165. Eleazer,[6] b. 1793, 3. 14. (*Vide infra.*)

166. Stephen,[6] b. 1796, 3. 11; m. March 13, 1821. Abigail, dau. of Daniel Shehane, of Salem. She d. Aug. 6, 1844, æt. forty-one. He d. at Liverpool, Eng., Jan. 25, 1837.

167. Gertrude,[6] b. 1799, 8. 14; m. Dec. 26, 1822, Jona. Barrett, b. at Salem, Dec. 11, 1790, and d. April 18, 1829; had Eleazer Pope, b. Sept. 29, 1824; Martha Osborn, b. July 9, 1827.

(108)

FOLGER POPE,[5] b. at Salem, 1756, 2. 14, a saddler, shop on Washington street, opposite City Hall; m. Theodate, who was born at Salem, 1759, 1. 1. Children, —

168. Folger,[6] b. 1782, 9. 18, at Salem.

169. Stephen,[6] b. 1784, 1. 11, at Salem. (*Vide infra.*)

170. Lydia,[6] b. 1785, 10. 31, at Salem.

171. Daniel,[6] b. 1787, 11. 11, at Salem.

172. Hannah,[6] b. 1789, 12. 28.

(111)

JOSHUA POPE,[5] b. 1763, 11. 24; d. 1842, 2. 25, a tanner in Salem; first, m. Bethiah, dau. of   Dean. She was born 1764, d. 1817, 2. 14; m. secondly, Lucretia, the widow of I. Johnson, and dau. of Zach. and Lucretia Collins, of Lynn. She was born at Lynn, and died at Salem, July 21, 1856, aged eighty-one.

173. Jonathan Dean,[6] b. 1792, 8. 8.; d. 1846.

174. Gertrude,[6] b. 1794, 9. 6; d. 1796, 10.

175. James,[6] b. 1797, 3. 12; d. June 6, 1852; a tanner, lived in Salem; m. Lucy M., dau. of Capt. Daniel Lord, of Ipswich. She died Nov. 29, 1823, æt. twenty-one.

176. Peter,[6] b. 1799, 6. 25; d. 1803, 7. 5.

177. Lot,[6] b. 1803, 4. 27; d. at Salem, April 8, 1859, tanner. His

wife, Maria, d. at Salem, June 9, 1842, aged twenty-nine.

(112)

James Pope,[5] b. Dec. 16, 1765; d. 1830, 8. 7, saddler, place of business on Federal street, near Baptist Meeting-House ; m. Lydia, dau. of Daniel and Hannah Newhall. She was b. at Lynn. 1775, 3. 16; d. at Salem, 1830, 12. 8.

178. James,[5] b. 1795, 3. 6; d. 1796, 3. 11.

179. Hannah,[6] b. 1797, 2. 15; d. 1843, 1. 18.

180. James,[6] b. 1799, 7. 21; d. 1800, 12. 24.

181. Daniel,[6] b. 1801, 11. 30; d. at Milwaukie. Aug. 10, 1852.

182. Mary Ann,[6] d. May 13, 1852, aged forty-four.

183. Lydia,[6] b. 1808, 2. 27.

184. James,[6] b. 1810, 7. 25; d. 1834, 7. 9, at Tobasco, Mexico.

185. Elizabeth Hacker,[6] b. 1813. 3. 17.

186. Joseph,[6] b. 1816, 8. 22; d. 1820, 9. 22.

187. Sarah Nichols,[6] b. 1821, 6. 2.

(118)

John Pope,[5] of Boston, b. 1740, 10. 29; m. Hannah, dau. of James and Sarah Raymar, of Boston; b. 1743-4, 12. 16.

188. John,[6] b. at Boston, 1769, 4. 8.

189. James,[6] b. at Boston, 1770, 12. 25.

190. Hannah,[6] b. at Boston, 1772, 8. 13.

191. Benjamin,[6] b. at Boston, 1774, 6. 11; d. 1774, 8. 24.

192. Sarah,[6] b. at Boston, 1775, 8. 25.

193. Ruth,[6] b. at Boston, 1777, 9. 30.

194. Susanna,[6] b. at Boston, 1779, 10. 13.

195. Samuel,[6] b. at Boston, 1781, 9. 15.

196. Benjamin,[6] b. at Boston, 1783, 3. 3.

197. Betsey,[6] b. at Boston, 1786, 2. 7.

VI. GENERATION.

(134)

Nathaniel Pope,[6] yeoman, of Danvers, b. Aug. 2, 1792; m. Aug. 8, 1815, Abi Preston, b. Feb. 13, 1791; d. March 1, 1841; m. secondly, March 9, 1848, Charlotte. dau. of Elijah and Elizabeth (Putnam) Flint, of South Danvers. She was born May 12, 1801. Children, —

198. Elizabeth Putnam,[7] b. Feb. 12, 1816; m. Andrew M. Putnam, of Danvers.

199. Harriet Adeline,[7] b. Sept. 8, 1817; m. Henry F. Putnam, of Danvers.

200. Mary Putnam,[7] b. July 26, 1819; m. Calvin Putnam, of Danvers.

201. Aseneth Preston,[7] b. Sept. 19, 1821; m. Nathan Tapley, of Danvers.

202. Ira Preston,[7] b. Sept. 11, 1823 ; m. Eliza C. Batchelder.

203. Daniel Putnam.[7] b. March 8, 1826 ; m. Lydia X. Dempsey.

204. Hannah Putnam,[7] b. June 2, 1828 ; m. Dr. B. Breed, of Lynn.

205. Phebe Mansfield,[7] b. May 12, 1830 ; d. Aug. 29, 1830.

206. Jasper Felton.[7] b. April 4, 1832 ; m. Sophia J. Richards, of Townsend.

(138)

JASPER POPE,[6] b. July 14, 1802 ; m. Dec. 13, 1830. Harriet Felton. She was born Sept. 19, 1803 ; d. Nov. 24, 1843. He m. secondly, Feb. 9, 1846, Sarah Felton. She was born Jan. 4, 1807, had —

207. Jasper Elijah,[7] b. Feb. 12, 1847.

(140)

ELIJAH POPE,[6] b. July 13, 1809 ; m. December, 1831. Eunice Prince. She was born May 19, 1811.

208. Francis Elijah,[7] b. May 29, 1832.

209. Nathaniel A.,[7] b. Dec. 24, 1837.

210. Samuel Putnam,[7] b. Dec. 16, 1844.

211. Mary Elizabeth,[7] b. June 14, 1847.

212. James Arthur,[7] b. July 29, 1817 ; d. Jan. 9, 1852.

(141)

ZEPHANIAH POPE,[6] yeoman, of Danvers. b. Dec. 15, 1807 : m. April 9,
1835, Nancy Mudge ; b. at Danvers, June 9, 1816. Children, —

213. Amos Alden,[7] b. at Danvers, Feb. 16, 1838 ; d. at Danvers, Sept. 15, 1864.

214. Sarah Ann,[7] b. at Danvers. May 5, 1842.

215. Caroline Eunice.[7] b. at Danvers. Feb. 2, 1847.

(161)

SAMUEL CARROLL POPE,[6] b. at Salem, Nov. 25, 1783 ; d. at Salem. Jan. 2, 1821 ; m. at Londonderry, Dec. 23, 1806, Frances Dinsmore, of Londonderry, dau. of Capt. Thomas Dinsmore. She was born in Boston, Sept. 28, 1785 ; d. in South Danvers, March 25, 1858.

He was a baker by trade. In 1807 was elected the first commander of the Salem Mechanic Light Infantry. but declined the position. In 1808. he was a Lieutenant in the Salem Artillery Company. Soon after the commencement of the war of 1812. he entered the U. S. service, and was 1st Lieutenant in the 40th Regiment of Infantry, and was stationed at Fort Gurnet. Plymouth. (See Vol. III. of these Collections, p. 181.) Children, —

216. Ann Hall,[7] b. Nov. 13, 1807. at Salem ; d. Nov. 3, 1831. at Salem. unm.

217. Samuel Lysander.[7] b. Jan. 20, 1809 ; d. July 29, 1829. at sea, off the coast of Timor. on board of ship Zephyr.

218. Orlando Ebenezer,[7] b. March 17, 1810, at Salem, now resident of South Danvers; m. June, 1832, Rebecca S. Fairfield, dau. of Moses and Elizabeth Fairfield, of Salem. She was born April 10, 1810. Children born at Danvers,— Frances P., b. Dec. 19, 1832; Orlando Lysander, b. Dec. 10, 1834; d. Oct. 11, 1839; George Stephen, b. July 29, 1836; d. Sept. 6, 1839; Elizabeth Mehitable, b. Sept. 11, 1838; Orlando George, b. July 29, 1840; d. Dec. 6, 1840; George O. H., b. Oct. 5, 1844; Ellen M., b. Sept. 4, 1848.

219. Frances Dinsmore, b. Dec. 25, 1811; m. Stephen Palmer. of Lynn, Aug. 22, 1833. He died.

She and her son, William L. Palmer, reside now in Salem. He served the country with honor during the recent rebellion. At the first call for troops, he went as a private in the Salem Light Infantry, April 18, 1861, and served three months in that capacity. At the organization of the 19th Reg. Mass. Vols. in August, 1861, he received the appointment of 2d Lieut.; 1st Lieut., June 18, 1862; April 16, 1863, Capt.; April 8, 1865, Major; March 13, 1865, Brevet Lieut. Colonel.

220. Mehitable Carroll,[7] b. Dec. 2, 1815.

(165)

ELEAZER POPE,[6] b. at Salem, 1793, 3. 14. Tanner, m. May 24, 1818, Mary Nimblet, dau. of Robert Nimb-

let, of Salem. She died May, 1822; he m. secondly, April 27, 1823, Esther Reith, dau. of Capt. John Reith, of Salem. Children,—

221. Henry E.,[7] b. Feb. 16, 1819; during the recent war was an assistant surgeon in the 6th Reg. Indiana Vols.; now resides in Salem; m. May 18, 1856, Catherine M., dau. of Munroe W. and Mary (Dole) Lee. She was b. at Madison, Ind., and d. at Salem, April 24, 1866, æt. thirty, having had William H., b. Feb. 22, 1857, and Charles S., b. Sept. 1, 1858.

222. William A,[7] a tanner, of Salem, b. April 18, 1820; m. Elizabeth, dau. of Alexander and Jane McCloy, Oct. 31, 1844; she d. June 6, 1847, aged twenty-three; he m. secondly, Mary D. Symonds, Sept. 25, 1852. Children,—William H., b. May 26, 1845, d. Aug. 8, 1845; William H., b. April 14, 1847; Mary E., b. March 7, 1853; George, b. Jan. 7, 1855; Frank A., b. March 27, 1857, d. Jan. 2, 1861.

223. Mary,[7] b. April, 1822; m. Lorenus Warner, of South Danvers; she died October, 1852, having had Mary E., b. April 8, 1852.

224 John R.,[7] a tanner, of Salem, b. Sept. 4, 1824; m. Mary J. Brown. Children,—Esther, b. Sept. 11, 1849; John H., b. Jan. 30, 1852; Mary Jane, b. July 21, 1854; Stephen F., b. Feb. 14, 1858. He died Nov. 22, 1861.

2*

225. Esther,[7] b. Nov. 28, 1826 m. Jan. 1, 1854, Andrew Mace; she died June, 1855.

226. Stephen,[7] b. Nov. 28, 1828.

227. James,[7] b. 1830; d. 1831.

228. James,[7] b. March 29, 1839. July 6, 1761, he was commissioned 1st Lieut. 1st Reg. Heavy Artillery, Mass. Vols.; Capt., June 10, 1862, discharged Oct. 18, 1864, resides in Salem.

229. Frank,[7] b. Jan. 18, 1841; m. Sarah Morison, Nov. 30, 1865; he was commissioned 2d Lieut., 1st Reg. Heavy Artillery, Mass. Vols., Feb. 15, 1862; 1st Lieut., March 19, 1863, discharged on expiration of service. Oct. 7, 1864; Capt., March 17, 1865. He died Dec. 28, 1866.

(169)

STEPHEN POPE,[6] b. 1784, 1. 11; m. Sally   : b. 1788, 8. 7.
Children. —

230. Daniel,[7] b. 1808. 11. 4.
231. Sarah,[7] b. 1811. 1. 11.
232. Mary,[7] b. 1813, 7. 21.
233. Seba,[7] b. 1816, 3. 9.
234. Abel H.,[7] b. 1825. 4. 13.
235. George F.,[7] b. 1827, 3. 23; d. 1828, 2. 8.

www.ingramcontent.com/pod-product-compliance
Lightning Source LLC
Chambersburg PA
CBHW031156090426
42738CB00008B/1364